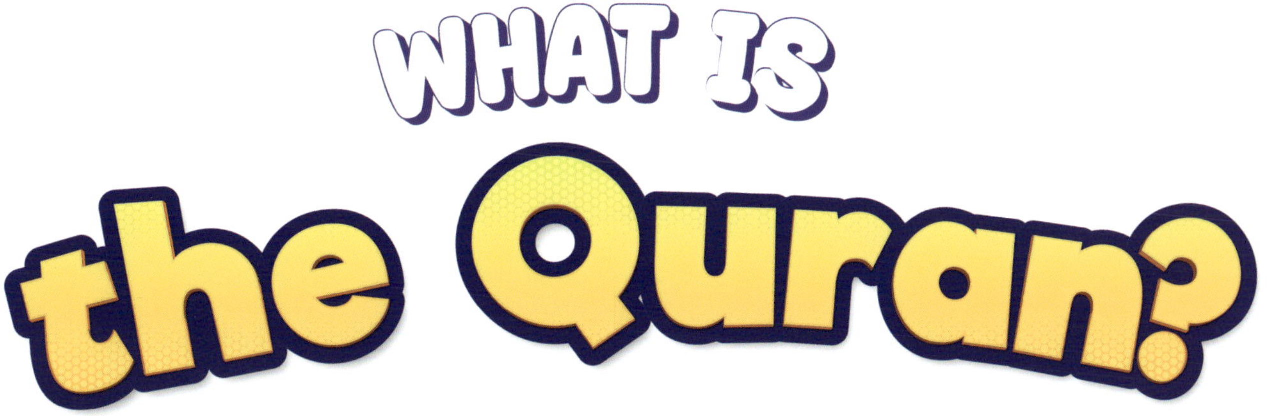

This book belongs to:

____

24 23 22 21 1 2 3 4

Published by Tughra Books
335 Clifton Ave.
Clifton, NJ, 07011, USA
www.tughrabooks.com

ISBN: 979-8-89729-503-6

Mini Muslims Series ISBN 9781597849692

WHAT IS the Quran?

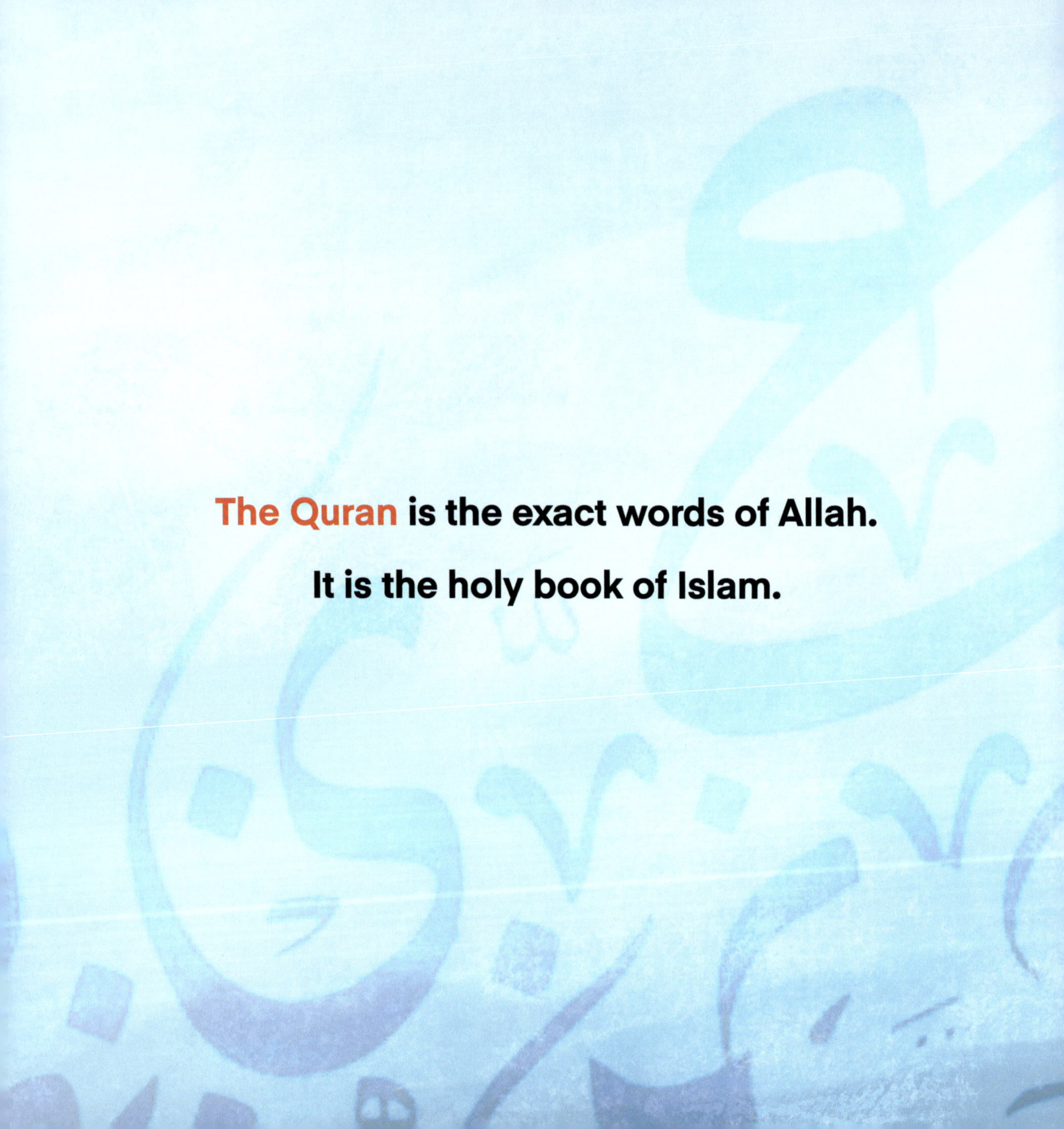

The Quran is the exact words of Allah.

It is the holy book of Islam.

It was sent down from Allah to
the Prophet Muhammad (pbuh).

It teaches us about Allah and how to worship Him.

It shows us what is right and wrong.

It tells us stories so we can learn from them.

The Quran is a guide for all people on how to live.

We love to learn the Quran and teach it to others!

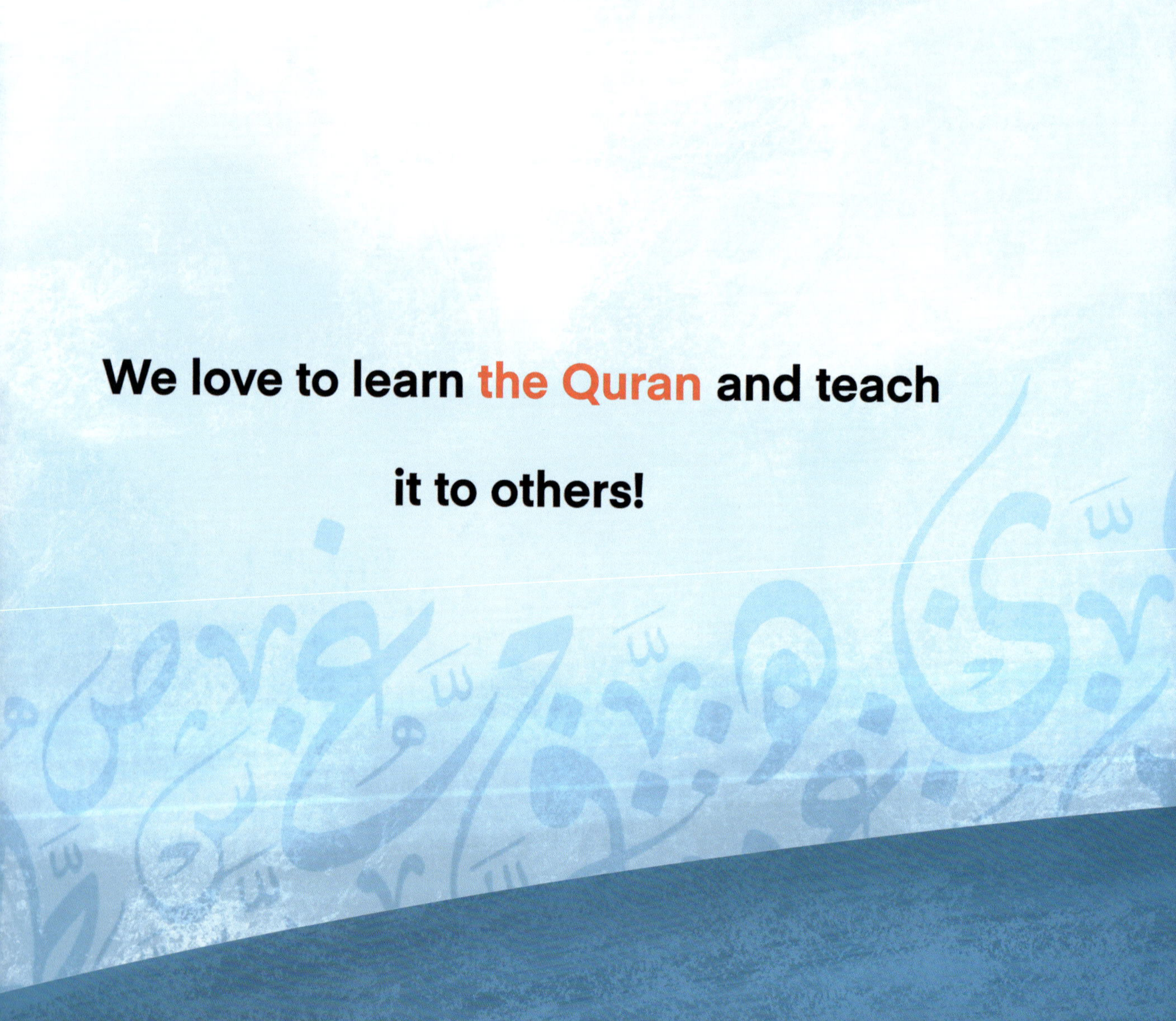